THE MISSING

WILL KEMP

Published by Cinnamon Press
Meirion House,
Glan yr afon,
Tanygrisiau
Blaenau Ffestiniog,
Gwynedd, LL41 3SU
www.cinnamonpress.com

The right of Will Kemp to be identified as author of this work has been asserted by him in accordance with the Copyright, Designs and Patent Act, 1988. Copyright © 2015 Will Kemp
ISBN: 978-1-907090-59-1
British Library Cataloguing in Publication Data. A CIP record for this book can be obtained from the British Library.
All rights reserved. No part of this publication may be reproduced, stored in a retrieval system, or transmitted in any form or by any means, electronic, mechanical, photocopying, recording or otherwise without the prior written permission of the publishers. This book may not be lent, hired out, resold or otherwise disposed of by way of trade in any form of binding or cover other than that in which it is published, without the prior consent of the publishers.
Designed and typeset in Palatino by Cinnamon Press
Cover design by Jan Fortune
Printed in Poland
Cinnamon Press is represented in the UK by Inpress Ltd and in Wales by the Welsh Books Council

Acknowledgments

Thanks to the editors of journals in which these and other poems have appeared: *Acumen, Aesthetica, Ambit, Angle, Cake, Envoi, Equinox, Essence, Fourteen, The French Literary Review, The Guardian, Haiku Quarterly, The Interpreter's House, Iota, The Journal, Magma, The New Writer, The North, Obsessed with Pipework, Orbis, Other Poetry, Poetry News, Poetry Scotland, The Rialto, The SHOp, Smith's Knoll.*

Thanks too to Carole Bromley, Doreen Gurrey, Ann and Peter Sansom, Susan Richardson, Molly Donachie, Carol-Ann Duffy, Helen, Ged, Jackie, Dave, Jan and everyone at Cinnamon.

And a special thanks to John and Elisabeth, for providing the way that led to the light, and to Sibylle, for so much colour.

The Missing Girl: after *The Missing Boy* by the Durutti Column, Factory Records, 1981.

About the Author

Will Kemp has won the Envoi International Poetry Prize (2010), the Cinnamon Press Debut Poetry Collection Award (2010) and the Cinnamon Pamphlet Competition (2014). He has also come second in the Keats-Shelley Prize (2013) and The Poetry Society's Stanza Competition (2011). Cinnamon Press published his first two collections, *Nocturnes* (2011) and *Lowland (2013),* and will publish his third, *Study of Clouds*, in 2015. He lives near York and works as an environmental planner.

Contents

The Misssing Girl

I. Disquiet	7
II. Distress	8
III. Fall	9
IV. Shawl	10
V. Arethusa	12
VI. Hell	14
VII. Lost	15
VIII. Judgement	16
IX. Resolve	17
X. Snowscene	18
XI. Revenge	19
XII. Aftermath	20
XIII. Release	22
XIV. Return	23

The Missing Girl

for Kathy,
wherever she is

I. Disquiet

Silent, slow, the woods and fields
a sage and mustard scene.

The old ash tree olive-grey,
that larch pale yellow, *sfumato*,

as if veiled in mist or woodsmoke,
yet there was no fire to be seen.

Strange, this – for up until now,
green had always been green.

II. Distress

Demeter found it odd there'd been rain:
the plain was watered the week before –
none was due at all today.

Odd too there was no laughter
at the clearing. It must be a game:
soon she'd hear a twig crack, a giggle
behind a shrub. But today just grazing deer.
Where was Persephone?

Demeter called her name.

No answer came.

The meadow where they danced,
that's where she'd be – walking through
field after ripening field,
a hand trailing over ears of corn.

Instead, some flowers lay scattered
about the path. A harmless chase perhaps,
or something else? Her mind raced:
hunters, fauns – *no, anything but that.*

Demeter called her name.

Again, and again, and again.

But still no answer came.

III. Fall

Nothing made sense anymore.
The girl gone, the trees as well:

the elm now amber over lime;
a plane lemon, as if acid-dipped;

maples blushing, that cherry too –
pale red against the brilliant blue.

Others rusting, charred ochre:
the oak somehow a faded master,

that chestnut threadbare,
leaves like rags on a damp floor.

And then the birch – a shower
of dots like trailing cinders.

Look out, it seemed to say,
I die in flames. Winter is already here.

IV. Shawl

There, by the river, with patterns of flowers, vines –
Persephone's since she was a girl.

Demeter held it as if cradling a sleeping child –
hands closed like buds, mouth a little o –
at once breathed in hibiscus, jasmine, rose;
recalled those first steps in the lemon grove.

Fruit. Persephone always loved fruit.
Apple, melon, plum: names learnt by heart,
practised like a song. Bluebell, primrose too,
all those questions on how leaves and petals grow.

In no time she flourished: took cuttings from ash
and willow; could paint a green field yellow.

A natural, down-to-earth too – laughed
as she sprinkled seeds, helped ladybirds to leaves.

Just couldn't be kept in: would follow
the flight of swallows over hills, vales, fields,
forever finding new paths and streams.

But she'd return.

The one time she did go missing, Demeter found
her on ground lit blue by the moon – decided
then to make the shawl (even though
in truth the girl was always a little hot);

at once Persephone draped it round and hugged
her mother – then promptly asked
if she could now stay out till dawn.

If she would only answer her name,
Demeter could hold her again – touch that head
the way cows nudge their young to water.

Instead, she stared at the river, remembering
stories, dances, walks:
her smile, her songs, her warmth.

V. Arethusa

A splash.
And then another,
as a pale-skinned girl
with jaded eyes walked
calmly from the water –
waxen face a stare,
threaded reeds for hair,
her voice no more
than a murmur:

You must be the mother.
I know by the way
you hold the shawl.

I saw it all:
the deadened sky,
these waters recede
like a tide sucked back to sea;
some dust rising far away,
that growing rumble,
then shouts, whip cracks,
the chariot's snorting team –
each muscle straining
in a sleek black gleam –
hooves drumming the ground,
coming like thunder –
Hades' one-armed hold
on the reins and screaming girl,
her stricken face glancing
back again and again,
his forked spear striking
the river – earth and water
at once ripped apart
in a streak of lightning.

And then the fall:
*   straight*
and headlong into Hell,
the great cleft hole
already closing as they fell,
water roaring in,
charging over
the charred and splintered seam,
drowning out
the snorts and shouts and screams.

VI. Hell

For Persephone,
day was now night,
a dripping dark
no god could light,
or lift the gloom
behind those eyes –
her drugged look
the joy he took
in that plunder –
his horses' hooves,
that roll of thunder –
snatched from paths,
streams, flowers
and outstretched arms –
then stripped
and fucked,
and fucked again,
by a man she should call uncle.

VII. Lost

Demeter sat in black
under a vine-clad trellis,
the sky unwanted blue.

Behind, scythes, seed
with no green tongues
poking through.

Ahead, scorched earth,
yellowed crops; trees
that brass and copper.

Stranger still, the river:
a dried up thread where
nothing stirred at all.

She looked on and on,
the singing water gone,
or somehow taken away.

VIII. Judgement

Zeus sat back on his marble throne,
gazing at the rock above the colonnade,
light rippling from the pool below.

Demeter, this drought must stop.
Everywhere bolted and withered crops,
thistles thrust up in parched fields,
choking coughs by empty troughs;
the hiss and crackle of locust swarms
stripping the standing corn,
forest fires torching hills and valleys.
And you take the word of a water spirit,
when Hades is our brother.
He will have his story too.
Do not ignore his lot in that tomb
with only the glimmer
of dark fire along its vaults,
that slow drip of water in the gloom.
And everywhere, cries, wails, groans;
lost faces, shadows, the sway
of sackcloth figures – hollow, grey –
like reeds on a river bed, serving
the drift of whatever current flows.
Hell is where no one goes.
Besides, Persephone is hardly a child;
yours, yes, but not yours to own.
The girl will adjust in time.
Think of the underworld
as a place for her to explore.
There is nothing you can do.

IX. Resolve

Outside, Demeter noted the chill,
recalled the coldness of his words.

The girl will adjust in time.
There is nothing you can do.

Not one fact established,
no questions asked – time, place,
abduction by brute force.

But of course: she only had to think
of Europa, Leda, the others; to him,
girls were for taking, raping.

What a fool she'd been to come.
Persephone hadn't even entered
the equation. And what appeal
could there be when he was king?

She'd never liked it there –
that smell of wine, the talk of war.
Out here was where she belonged.
Where she was strong.

X. Snowscene

pale sky   field hedges

slightly darker   like charcoal

lines on white paper

XI. Revenge

Demeter smiled at her work,
the world icebound, gone –
but this was only the start;
time now to turn the screw:
rain and meltwater –
nothing could be stronger
to make him relent and give.

At once icicles tinkled, glistened;
white giving way to grey –
a pulp revealing corpses
buried during the long siege –
whilst hollows began to trickle
into twisting streams of water
eager to find its own level.

And overhead, clouds bruising
to black, the sky a heaving sea.

XII. Aftermath

Zeus pleaded: *Demeter, please stop.*
First the drought, then ice and snow
before the rain – no fine drizzle
but huge monsoons pasting
the ground to slime, exposing
cliffs, drilling hills until they bleed
water to overloaded streams –
rivers gathering mud and speed,
churning brown as a single force
aimed at cities, towns, then hurled
full tilt at defenceless places
in avalanches of water – bursting
banks to sweep away houses, farms,
submerging lanes, fields and barns.

And now the wake: the land like fens,
flooded fields a shattered mirror,
floating with bloated bodies –
limbs of livestock like upturned tables –
sullied fields returned to marshes
of rotting crops and silted corpses –
drenched carrion for ravens, rats –
the countless dead strewn across
the ground as the sea breaks through
to over-run the wells and sewers.

Everywhere, streets sludged in mud
and shit, the stench souring the air –
houses feeding grounds for teeming flies,
the urban fringe a shanty town
where red-eyed women beg for food,
those not found, and orphaned children –
dank clothes clinging to blotched skin –
become urchins adept at looting.

*Better for them to have drowned
than live here – sea walls overtopped,
soil waterlogged to negate all crops –
in hopeless famine, disorder,
caught between extremes of weather,
forever, returned to a primal state,
but worse, having once known
health, love, fresh water.*

Why they must suffer I now see.

*So, if you desist, know this:
Persephone will be released from Hell
unless she has touched its fruit.*

*Please consider these terms for peace;
our power no match for yours.*

XIII. Release

Demeter could see it all:
Hermes in the dark realm
where nothing grows,
Hades' glower,
Persephone starting
the long ascent –
no looking back at rows
of ravens, crows,
that thick fog rolling
over the River Styx –
daylight starting to show –
the girl likening it
to rose then peach,
thinking how the sun was
an orange or a lemon –
the earth already sensing
that rising warmth,
each bud about to grow.

XIV. Return

Clouds billow, balloon,
laundry on a line,
then roll away,
a sailboat passing by.

Between showers,
a game of hide and seek:
blue giving way to grey
then back to blue again.

Through woods, fields,
a surge of life –
tiny shoots, trees opening
hands of leaves –

as at last she comes
into view, heading
waves of green, holding
the flowers of summer,

that smile fixed
on the mother who runs
to her crying out loud:
Just look at all we can do.